P9-EER-239

Smart

SOLUTIONS

FALL RIVER PRESS

Smartest Solution—**Subscribe to First Magazine and save 41%**
17 issues (one year) for just $19.97

Mail to:

First for Women
PO Box 1922
Marion, OH 43306-0822

Be sure to include your name, address and payment to First Magazine
OR
Online at www.myfirstforwomen.com

© 2006 by Fall River Press

First for Women magazine and the *First* logo are registered trademarks
of Bauer Publishing Company, L.P., and are used with permission.
Smart solutions © Bauer Publishing Company, L.P.

All rights reserved. No part of this publication may be reproduced,
stored in a retrieval system, or transmitted, in any form or by any means,
electronic, mechanical, photocopying, recording, or otherwise,
without prior written permission from the publisher.

Illustrations by Barbara McGregor

Fall River Press
122 Fifth Avenue
New York, NY 10011

ISBN: 978-0-7607-8282-8

Printed and bound in China

5 7 9 10 8 6 4

While every effort has been made to ensure the accuracy and completeness of the
information contained in this book, the publisher must disclaim all warranties,
expressed or implied, regarding the information. While the publisher does not believe
any information contained herein to be harmful, the publisher also cannot assume any
responsibility for use of this book, and any use by a reader is at the reader's own risk.

CONTENTS

FOREWORD

It happens to the smartest, most practical, and most prepared among us: a little problem that seems to defy solution. We're momentarily confounded—daunted by limitations of time (could we have any more to do?), of cash (could gas get any more expensive?) and, well, of sanity (could life get any crazier?). That's where Smart Solutions come in. Introduced ten years ago as a one-page department in *First for Women* magazine, Smart Solutions has been such a hit for *First*'s super-busy readers that it has grown to three full-fledged departments: "You," "Food," and "Home." And *First* readers consistently rank all three departments as the ones they love most in the magazine.

What makes Smart Solutions so irresistible? Reading them in advance of an impending chink in your womanly armor makes you feel invincible—and having a problem that's solved by a tiny tip makes you feel like you've won life's lottery (at least for an hour or so!). Here's what I mean: One night before a dinner party, the one bulb that lights my stovetop burned out. I dug up a Phillips-head screwdriver and carefully unscrewed the covering over the light bulb. (The screws were fussy and my angle was necessarily bizarre—picture a 40-year-old woman curled up half in the sink, half on the countertop, looking like a misguided Twister player.) Finally, the cover came off and I grabbed the light bulb. Big mistake. Little did I know, those years of sopping up grease and hot air had rusted the metal neck of the bulb and fused it with its housing. The result: the glass shattered into pieces and the rusted neck was stuck in place.

I was flooded with disappointment. I would have to reassemble the whole mess, clean up the glass, and then—and this was the part that really stung—fork over upwards of $100 for the pleasure of being inconvenienced by a tardy repairman. All for this dumb, rusted light-bulb neck! But then I remembered a Smart Solution we had run that advised wedging a raw potato into a light bulb casing and using it to unscrew the casing from within. Because the bulb had been so small, the potato didn't do the trick, but the tip got me thinking along the right lines, and when I substituted a balled-up piece of bread—eureka!—it worked!

The sense of relief and accomplishment, not to mention the savings, kept me buoyed for days (I still feel happy thinking about it), and that's what I hope this collection of Smart Solutions will do for you. These tips are fast, easy, and rely on inexpensive household heroes you already have on hand (no runs to the store required!). They're fixes to life's little problems, but they can make a big difference in how you feel about yourself and all you have to do. Adapt them to suit your needs, pass them along to help friends and neighbors, and give yourself a pat on the back for being the multitasking miracle-worker you truly are!

Carol Brooks
Editor in Chief, *First for Women*

Chapter 1

Mind & Body

WHEN YOU'RE BUSY, it's often hard to remember to take care of yourself. So if you don't have the time to treat yourself to a massage, a workout, or even just a soak in the tub, here are some quick tips to keep you motivated, rejuvenated, and ready to face the challenges ahead of you. From getting a deeper sleep to relieving tension headaches to learning to eat less, these how-tos for your mind and body will leave you feeling ready to handle whatever life throws your way.

The sleeping trick that soothes indigestion

NEXT TIME A LATE MEAL triggers sleep-stealing heartburn, lie on your left side. This positions the esophagus higher than the stomach, making it difficult for food and digestive acid to reflux back into the throat. The result: you can drift off without distress.

Stop summer sniffles with honey

DRIZZLE HONEY ON FOOD instead of sugar to keep sickness at bay. Its immunity-boosting anti-oxidants are as powerful as those in most fruits and vegetables.

No more late-night nibbling

To stave off a midnight snack attack, try this move: Sitting up in bed, extend the left leg and bend the right knee. Next, place your right hand at your side for balance and touch your left elbow to the outside of your right knee. Hold for three breaths and switch sides. The twisting motion of this yoga posture, called Marichyasana, functions as an internal abdominal massage that triggers the release of appetite-suppressing brain chemicals.

The stance
that spells success

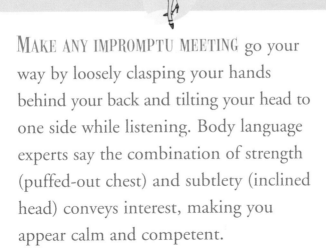

MAKE ANY IMPROMPTU MEETING go your way by loosely clasping your hands behind your back and tilting your head to one side while listening. Body language experts say the combination of strength (puffed-out chest) and subtlety (inclined head) conveys interest, making you appear calm and competent.

Outsmart a sneaky source of tiredness

YOU'RE STRUGGLING TO GET THROUGH your endless errand list when you find yourself exhausted and bleary-eyed. What gives? Maybe your sweater. According to a recent study, wool attracts 10 times more allergens than other fibers. That's because wool naturally absorbs moisture from the air, making it a magnet for airborne dust allergens. To keep your woolens from making you tired, simply throw them in the dryer on a low setting for 30 minutes once a week. The tossing and heat dislodge small particles from the wool fibers, leaving your sweaters allergen-free and you with lots of energy!

The stress zapper that lets you love what you do

IF DIFFICULTY CHANGING HATS (mom, wife, friend) means you get less than the most out of every moment, try this mini move when you're about to switch gears: Sit up straight, raise your arms to the sides, and bend your elbows so your forearms are perpendicular to the ground, fingers pointing upward. Next, spread your fingers and rotate your hands for two minutes by pivoting at the wrists. This hand move creates an energy vortex that draws anxiety out of the body, filling you with the serenity and stamina you need to relish every second of your day.

The secret to outsmarting restaurant calories

IT'S EASY TO OVERINDULGE when the size of the main course at your favorite restaurant is triple what you'd normally dish out at home. To keep from eating more than you truly want, munch on an apple before you leave the house. Apples are rich in pectin, a soluble fiber that slows the digestive process, so you'll feel full on less food. The result: you'll eat just enough to make you happy—and even have leftovers to bring home!

Soothe swimmer's ear

STOP THE PAIN OF SWIMMER'S EAR by mixing 2 teaspoons white vinegar with 2 teaspoons rubbing alcohol, then squeezing two drops into the affected ear with a cotton ball. Doctors say the alcohol helps evaporate the trapped water, while the vinegar's acidity stops infection by keeping bacteria from growing.

The scent that suppresses a sweet tooth

NEXT TIME A CHOCOLATE URGE has you in its grip, fend off the yen by smoothing on vanilla-scented hand cream. (Or take a whiff of vanilla extract if you don't have moisturizer.) Research shows that the bean's aroma works like chocolate to trigger the release of serotonin, a brain chemical that boosts mood and suppresses appetite. Plus, the coating of cream on your hands will make you less likely to nibble with your fingers. The result? You will sail past the candy stash without batting an eye.

Relief for pins and needles

TO BANISH THE UNCOMFORTABLE FEELING of your hands "falling asleep" during long drives or hours of surfing the Web, neurologists advise rocking the head slowly in a side-to-side (ear-to-shoulder) motion for one minute. This move loosens the levator scapulae muscles. Tension in these muscles can compress a nerve that runs to the hands, which is what causes the numbing sensation.

Fast earache soother

TO STOP THE DIZZYING OUCH of an earache, heat an onion half in the microwave for 2 minutes, or until warm but not hot. Wrap it in a soft cloth or paper towel, apply the flat side to your ear and hold for 15 minutes. The heated vegetable emits sulfur, an anti-inflammatory gas that easily penetrates the ear canal to relieve pressure and pain.

Nix nervousness with a stretch

PUT AN END TO PRE-PARTY JITTERS while you set up. Simply grasp the stem of a wine glass between your thumb and forefinger, extend your arm and hold it in front of you for 30 seconds. Then switch hands and repeat. The stretching and concentration required transform anxiety into energy, so you can celebrate stress-free.

Get a second wind!

IF THERE'S NO TIME TO NAP before you head out to tonight's bash, try this instant energizer: Sit on the floor and hug your knees to your chin. Keeping your spine rounded, rock back and forth 12 times. This yoga mini-move massages the back and neck, causing the feel-great hormone serotonin to be released. You get the lift you need to party with the best of 'em!

Deep sleep— guaranteed

HAVING TROUBLE SLEEPING? Instead of popping a sleep aid that leaves you groggy the next day, try this trick: Drink half a glass of water, then put a pinch of salt on your tongue and let it dissolve, making sure the granules don't press against the roof of your mouth. Studies have shown that the combination of water and salt alters the electrical charge of the brain, inducing a deep slumber that helps take the edge off daytime stress.

Wake up happy!

ON CHILLY MORNINGS when jumping out of bed seems daunting, try this simple stretch: Sit upright with legs crossed and hands at your sides. Next, inhale as you lift your arms out and up, palms skyward, until they meet above your head; hold for three seconds. On the exhale, lower your elbows slowly to your sides. Repeat three times. This yoga pose, called Sun Celebration, improves breathing and blood flow to muscles, energizing the nervous system so you feel instantly invigorated.

Press here to delay hunger

IF THE BACKYARD GRILL GOES ON THE FRITZ, postponing dinner and leaving you ravenous, press the index and middle fingers of both hands three finger-widths below each knee along the outside of your legs. Stimulating these acupressure points, called the Sea of Nourishment, for 10 seconds stabilizes stomach activity to quell hunger pangs. You'll be able to hold out until mealtime without resorting to a predinner snack.

Erase airport stress

To stop long lines and pushy people from ruining your traveler's high, think about those who help you get from point A to point B—everyone from the pilots to the ticket agents. Remembering to think grateful thoughts makes you less defensive and more open to surprising new solutions.

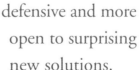

Chew away car sickness

IF YOU (OR YOUR LITTLE ONES) are prone to nausea during road trips, keep a pack of peppermint gum handy. The natural oils in peppermint help ease the queasies by slowing stomach contractions.

Beat drive-time drowsiness

IF YOUR REGULAR CIRCUIT of running errands leaves you pooped, hang a cinnamon-scented air freshener from your rearview mirror. A recent study found that subjects exposed to the aroma of cinnamon while driving stayed more alert and experienced considerably less fatigue than those exposed to no scent at all.

Bye-bye, post-lunch slumps

FOR A NO-FAIL WAY TO COMBAT SLUGGISHNESS and boost productivity during the inevitable afternoon energy dip, use the last 15 minutes of your lunch break to catch up with a coworker or a pal over the phone. Research shows that engaging in nonwork-related, lighthearted gossip relieves tension and bolsters morale, leaving you able—and inspired—to perform at your peak until the day's end.

The 5-second trick to making your best decision

JUST CAN'T MAKE UP YOUR MIND? Stand up and let your head and shoulders roll slowly toward the floor. With eyes open and arms hanging freely, hold the position for one minute as you breathe deeply. Hanging upside down literally gives you a "new world view" that's like a breath of fresh air for the brain. You'll see your situation in a different light and know what to do in a snap.

Relieve headaches— instantly!

NEXT TIME YOUR HEAD IS POUNDING, try this tension-tamer: Grab a small chunk of hair and gently tug and twist for two or three seconds. Repeat all over your head to stimulate blood flow to the scalp, easing the pain immediately.

The little secret to achieving your big dreams

UPLOAD PHOTOS OF FRIENDS AND FAMILY to use as screen savers on your computer. Research shows that images of loved ones spark the alpha and beta brainwave activity that promotes both calm and alertness. You'll be able to tackle the toughest projects with ease, wowing the boss, and maybe even landing that raise!

Outsmart tension headaches

TRAPPED TENSION IN THE MOUTH and throat area can lead to a throbbing headache. To dodge the pain (or relieve it when it does strike), suck on a Popsicle or an ice cube for a few minutes. This relaxes muscles, warding off stress-induced head pain and leaving you refreshed, reenergized, and raring to go!

Ease aches with pineapple

SAVOR 4 OUNCES OF PINEAPPLE whenever your muscles are achy. The fruit contains bromelain, an anti-inflammatory enzyme that helps repair injured muscle tissue.

Relief for eyestrain

ARE LONG HOURS IN FRONT OF A COMPUTER SCREEN straining your eyes? Preserve your vision with this simple exercise: Hold one thumb in front of you at arm's length. Move it in a circular motion for 30 seconds, then use it to trace figure eights for 30 seconds, all the while following your thumb with your eyes. This strengthens the orbital muscles that control eye movement, keeping your vision sharp.

The shower trick that makes you smarter

KEEP YOUR EYES CLOSED AS YOU take your morning shower. Using your sense of touch to find the soap and to shampoo your hair reawakens nerve cells in the brain's cortex, which controls memory. You'll start the day feeling sharp enough to master any situation!

A spicy way to alleviate stomach pain

SPRINKLING RED PEPPER on your plate can actually ward off indigestion. Study subjects who had 2.5 grams (about $1/2$ teaspoon) of red pepper powder before their meals had 48 percent fewer digestive symptoms than those who didn't pop the peppers.

One second to polish and poise

SPRITZ A LITTLE HAIRSPRAY on an old toothbrush and run it over unruly brows. The bristles groom, while the spray holds every hair in place so you look perfectly polished, professional, and in control from morning to night. (Just be sure to rinse the brush with hot water after each use.)

60 seconds to bliss!

WHEN STOMACH BUTTERFLIES STRIKE, sit down, place your left hand on your lower abdomen and your right hand over your heart, then close your eyes and breathe deeply for 60 seconds. Acupressure experts say this makes anxiety melt as the tension blocking energy channels between the heart and the kidneys is released, so you can keep your cool anytime, anywhere.

Tap to keep from blowing your lid

WHEN YOUR CHILD'S WHINING has hit on your last nerve, keep your cool with this acupressure trick: Using the tip of your index finger, lightly tap the crown of your head in one place while breathing deeply for 30 seconds. The body's energy channels converge at the top of the head, so stimulating the area sends relaxation signals to all your muscles. Tension will melt away, leaving you with the patience to tame a rambunctious tot.

SOS for menstrual pain

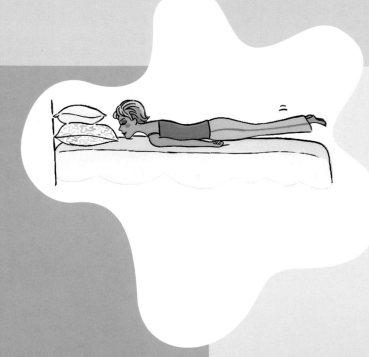

NEXT TIME PERIOD CRAMPS cost you
precious minutes of sleep, try this: Lie
on your stomach with your legs together
and chin on the mattress. Clench your
hands into fists and place them under
your hip bones. Inhale as you lift your
legs a few inches and hold for 30 seconds,
then lift them a little higher and hold
for 10 seconds; lower slowly. This yoga
move, called the Locust Pose, stimulates
a series of acupressure points that balance
the flow of energy through the lower
abdominal region, relaxing muscles and
soothing cramps so you can fall back
asleep in seconds.

File away your worries

To nix the stuff that gnaws at you—like that job you didn't get or your mother-in-law's offhand comment—jot it down on a scrap of paper, then stash it in a folder marked "Healing." The act of filing it sends a signal to your brain that you are done with the thought, and you can move on happy and worry-free.

Quiet stomach rumbles—instantly!

WHEN AN UNSCHEDULED MEETING puts your lunch hour on hold, silence a hungry tummy with this acupressure move: Using your thumb, massage the point halfway between your navel and breastbone by tracing tiny circles for 10 seconds. Stimulating this spot, which connects directly to the hypothalamus (the brain's appetite control center), creates a feeling of fullness that stops embarrassing growls in seconds.

Forget pesky worries

WHEN NAGGING CONCERNS are keeping you from focusing on the situation at hand, stand on one leg for a minute. Since the brain must process a large amount of sensory input to maintain balance, doing this instantly blocks out other distractions, allowing you to channel your thoughts and rise to even the toughest challenge.

Easy-on-you care for a sick child

NEXT TIME YOUR LITTLE ANGEL is home with the sniffles, make both of your lives easier by putting some walkie-talkies to work. Place one of them next to her bed and keep the other with you. This way, she can page you when she really needs you, and you can monitor her cough and tackle your must-dos at the same time.

Join a group effortlessly

TO EASE YOUR WAY INTO A CONVERSATION at a party where you hardly know anyone, try this: Stand nearby and smile at the dominant speaker. Recognizing the leader lets her know that you understand the group's dynamics. Being on the sidelines also gives the rest of the circle a chance to get used to you, prompting them to shift positions so you can join in.

The cushion trick that makes you feel full faster

AS YOU SIT DOWN TO DINNER, place a cushion between the small of your back and the chair. The pillow ensures you sit upright, a posture proven to help food travel faster to the lower stomach, causing "I'm full" signals to reach the brain in record time. You'll feel satisfied more quickly and whittle your waistline without even realizing it.

Wriggle away work woes

WHEN YOU FINALLY MAKE IT HOME after a tough day at the office, slip off your shoes and socks and walk across your plushest carpet, shuffling your feet as you go. The textured surface stimulates pressure points on the soles, triggering the release of calming hormones that make work headaches a distant memory and set the stage for a relaxing evening.

Say good-bye to stress

FOR A QUICK ANTIDOTE to tough situations, stash a rolling pin in your desk drawer. The next time your workday gets rough, just slip off your shoes and roll your feet over the pin for five minutes. This reflexology move triggers the release of endorphins, happiness-inducing brain chemicals that erase anxiety and give you the confidence to nail all your projects like a pro.

The tunes that turn off hunger

To INDULGE IN MOUTHWATERING FOOD without packing on the pounds, simply pop some slow music into the CD player during dinner. Research shows that subjects who dined to relaxing music ate 40 percent less than those who listened to faster songs—probably because they subconsciously mimicked the slow beat.

The finger tap that tames irritation

STUCK IN A TRAFFIC JAM? To keep your cool as the car inches ahead, place your middle finger ¼ inch above the mid-point between your eyebrows and tap lightly for 10 seconds. Stimulating this acupressure point, called Yingtan, lets you soothe tension without taking your eyes off the road, guaranteeing you'll be in a ready-for-anything frame of mind by the time you reach your destination.

Speed through to-dos

IF YOU JUST CAN'T FOCUS on your long list of chores, try this refocusing trick: Hold your hands so each thumb rests just below your rib cage and the fingers of both hands meet at your spine. Massage the area for 30 seconds. Practitioners of Qigong (a Chinese art that uses the body's energy to heal) say that stimulating this area prompts the kidneys to cleanse the body of toxins, boosting your productivity.

Score one against hunger

BEFORE ACCEPTING SECONDS of your favorite dish, rate how hungry you are on a scale of 1 (very hungry) to 7 (very full) and decline the offer if you score a 5 or above. (Try to stay between 3 and 5 so you're not starving and not stuffed.) Called mindful eating, this Zen technique connects you to your body's satiety signals so you know when to say "no thanks."

Eliminate nighttime leg cramps

SWOLLEN, ACHY LEGS keeping you up at night? Sidestep the pain with this yoga pose: A half hour before bedtime, lie on your back with legs flat against a wall, forming an L shape with your body; hold for 1 minute. Running around during the day can make calf muscles swell, impeding blood flow when you're horizontal and causing cramps. But elevating the legs eases fluid buildup, reducing inflammation and letting you enjoy a night of uninterrupted rest.

The spa secret for taming tension

WHEN A HECTIC DAY LEAVES YOU FRAZZLED and fussy, summon serenity with this water-therapy trick: Draw a hot bath and fill a squeeze bottle with lukewarm water. In the tub, drizzle the contents on your face in a clockwise motion; repeat five times. The waterfall-like sensation slows activity in the brain's hippocampus, where stressful memories are stored. Plus, it just feels terrific!

Never miss a chance to shine!

AT YOUR NEXT OFFICE BRAINSTORMING meeting, instead of blurting out the first thing you think of, wait for someone to offer an idea, then pause three seconds before responding. The break lets the cerebral cortex fully process the information so you can come at the suggestion from a different angle and devise even more inspired ideas.

Have your next eureka moment right now!

DRAWING A BLANK? Visualize an empty pitcher. Envisioning emptiness creates a space for new ideas in the cerebral cortex, the brain's problem-solving center. In a matter of moments, you'll be inspired with your next flash of genius!

Relieve back pain-
pronto!

TO KEEP AN ACHING BACK from slowing you down, try this move when pain strikes: Stand 3 feet from a wall, bend forward and place your hands against the wall at waist level. (Your back should be flat and parallel to the floor.) This stretches the spine and the trapezius muscle that runs from the neck to the shoulders, soothing aches in seconds.

Chapter 2

Fashion & Beauty

IF YOU'RE FEELING FRAZZLED you're not alone! After all today's woman has to do in the morning, who has time for hair, makeup, and clothes? Luckily, with these helpful hints, clingy skirts and smudged lipstick will be things of the past. You'll also learn how to make blemishes disappear faster, get your shoes shinier, and even make your pantyhose last longer—leaving you with more time before you have to dash out the door.

Fast fix for perfume overload

WHEN YOU ACCIDENTALLY BLAST YOURSELF with too much perfume just before you're about to dash out the door, tone down the fragrance with this quick trick: Simply rub a bit of unscented body lotion over the areas where you applied the perfume. The lotion absorbs and neutralizes scent molecules on the skin's surface so you can step out on time, leaving just the right amount of bouquet in your wake.

Erase pimples overnight

BEFORE YOU GO TO BED, dab a drop of diaper-rash ointment, like Desitin, on blemishes. The zinc oxide in the product dries excess oil and kills bacteria before they spread, ensuring your a.m. complexion is smooth, clear and radiating confidence.

The secret to fluffier cashmere

IT FIGURES: YOU'RE RUNNING LATE, and the cashmere sweater you plan to wear to tonight's dinner party emerges from your dresser looking slightly forlorn. The

fix? Pop it into a plastic bag and place it in the freezer for 30 minutes. The cold causes the hair fibers to expand, so you'll have a plush party-ready sweater by the time you've showered.

Wipe away winter shoe woes

WHEN SALT STAINS threaten your favorite pair of pumps, vinegar can save the day. Just apply a quarter-size amount of the liquid to a clean, soft washcloth and buff the streaky spots. The acetic acid breaks down salt crystals to wipe out white residue so it won't cramp your style.

Whisk away
self-tanner marks

TO ELIMINATE THE UNSIGHTLY STAINS left behind when sunless tanner seeps into the tiny crevices of knuckles and cuticles and the spaces between fingers and toes, moisten a cotton ball with nail polish remover and lightly swipe the affected areas. Ethyl acetate, the organic solvent in polish remover, dissolves excess product quickly and easily without leaving streaks, so you can show off your bronzed skin sans evidence of an application oops!

Bye-bye, ashy winter skin

CLEAR AWAY ANY TRACES of a dull, dry, cold-weather complexion with this homemade miracle: In a blender, puree 1 peeled kiwifruit and 1 1/2 teaspoons lime juice, then add an equal amount of water; pulse until smooth. Apply to your face with a cotton ball after cleansing skin. (Refrigerate leftovers in a sealed container for up to a week.) The vitamin C and other antioxidants in kiwifruit repair and rejuvenate skin, while the citric acid in the lime juice acts as a powerful exfoliant, leaving you with a captivating glow.

Never lose another button!

DAB CLEAR NAIL POLISH on each button of a new garment—front and back. This seals the threads, making pop-offs a thing of the past, so you always look (and feel!) pulled together.

Remove ink stains like magic!

SAY GOOD-BYE TO PESKY INK or marker stains on hands by adding a spoonful of sugar when you lather up. The slightly abrasive granules act as an exfoliant that successfully scrubs away marks in an instant.

Hide telltale gray roots in a flash!

NO TIME FOR A TOUCH-UP? Here's an instant fix for redheads and brunettes. Choose a mascara that closely matches your hair color and apply it to visible roots along the hairline. A quick blast from a blow-dryer sets the mascara so you get a fast shot of confidence until you have a chance to color.

Keep bras snag-free

TO PREVENT FINE WASHABLES like your best bras from hooking onto things in the washing machine (or even inside a mesh laundry bag), place them in a pillowcase and knot before tossing in. Your delicates will still be thoroughly cleaned, and the pillowcase will keep them from becoming torn or damaged during the cycle. Your silks and satins will emerge smelling fresh and looking flawless.

On-the-go cling cure

WHEN THAT SILKY SKIRT grabs your thighs and just won't let go, rub the positive end of a AA or AAA battery over it several times. (Store the battery in a sealed plastic bag in your purse.) Static cling is caused by a buildup of negatively charged electrons on fabric. But brushing them with the positively charged battery instantly neutralizes the electricity so you can step out without feeling self-conscious.

Uncover your inner glow— for free!

INSTEAD OF THROWING AWAY peels from limes, lemons, and oranges, slice them and store in a container in the fridge. Then come bath time, throw a handful into a tub of warm water. The heat of the bath releases a citrus scent that's been proven to invigorate, while the citric acid in the peels helps slough off dead skin cells to expose the soft, supple layer underneath.

Ouch-free bandage removal

INSTEAD OF STRIPPING off an adhesive bandage with a big "yeeeowch," set your hair dryer on low/warm and heat it for about 30 seconds. The sticky stuff melts away so removal is pain-free.

No more lipstick smudges!

RUN AN ICE CUBE OVER YOUR LIPS after applying lipstick. The ice sets the color and prevents it from bleeding or melting in the summer heat, ensuring a lasting smile that will make everyone's day.

Quick
bruise eraser

IF PLAYING OUTSIDE WITH THE KIDS has left you a little black-and-blue, apply a piece of banana peel (flesh side down) to the bruise, secure with a bandage, and leave on overnight. The gumlike substance in the peel, called mucilage, provides a protective barrier that helps bruises fade fast, so you don't have to worry about unsightly spots stealing attention from fabulous you!

Get clothes even cleaner!

IF YOUR CLOTHING ISN'T EMERGING from
the washer as spotless and as bright as it
used to, it's likely due to the accumulation
of soap scum in the washer hoses. To
dissolve, simply add 1 cup white vinegar
to an empty machine and run a small-
load cycle using the hot-water setting.
The acetic acid in vinegar dissolves
clog-causing buildup, so the washing
machine runs more smoothly and
clothes come out their absolute spiffiest.

Press out creases twice as fast

LAY A SHEET OF ALUMINUM FOIL (shiny side up) between the surface of your ironing board and its fabric cover. The foil reflects the iron's heat, so it smooths out wrinkles 200% faster!

Restore your gold's glitter

ADD 1 TEASPOON DISHWASHING LIQUID and 4 drops ammonia to 1 cup warm water. Dip dull or dirty gold rings, earrings, and bracelets into the solution and gently scrub with a nailbrush. Rinse in warm water, then dry and buff with a soft clean cloth. This potent mixture instantly cuts through buildup to bring back the precious metal's brilliance.

Make panty hose last 300% longer

GIVE YOUR HOSE A LIGHT SPRITZ of hairspray every time you put them on. The spray triples the nylon's lifespan by stiffening the fibers so they're less likely to get snagged or ripped.

Slip-proof your boots

GIVE SUPER-SLICK LEATHER SOLES extra grip by lightly rubbing them three times with sandpaper. The gritty toolbox staple will roughen the bottoms of your shoes, helping you avoid a nasty slip on icy winter sidewalks.

Easy razor-burn remedy

HAS SOAP-AND-WATER SHAVING left your legs red and stinging? This strategy offers instant relief: Apply a thin layer of plain yogurt to the affected area, let sit for three minutes, then rinse off with cool water and pat dry with a clean towel. The lactic acid in yogurt calms and soothes skin while gently exfoliating the top layer of irritated cells, easing the appearance of razor burn so you can bare your smooth legs in comfort.

The secret to shinier shoes

IF YOU SCUFF YOUR LEATHER PUMPS en route to a fancy event, spiff them up instantly with an item you're likely to have in your handbag: lip balm. Simply rub a dime-size dab on the front, back and both sides of each shoe, then gently buff with a tissue to get the surface shiny. The balm contains petrolatum, a wax-based ingredient that restores sheen, which means you can make a sparkling entrance.

Take the sting out of a paper cut

TO PREVENT A LITTLE PAPER CUT from turning into a daylong annoyance, dab a pencil eraser–size drop of nontoxic white glue, such as Elmer's, on the area. Once dry, the glue creates a hygienic barrier (just like a liquid bandage) to seal out air, dull the pain and allow the wound to heal without the risk of reopening.

GLUE

SOS for an untimely blemish

NEXT TIME A CONFIDENCE-SAPPING ZIT POPS UP right before an all-eyes-on-you presentation, try this: Apply an ice cube to the area for 30 seconds, then gently press a cotton pad soaked in eyedrops on the spot for three minutes. The ice and the drops cause blood vessels just beneath the skin's surface to contract, minimizing redness and irritation and refreshing your can-do spirit.

The secret to feeling comfortable in new jeans

YOU WANT TO SHOW OFF your brand-new jeans, but they're so stiff that sitting in them is unpleasant. To break them in fast, toss them in the dryer with three tennis balls and run on a low setting for 15 minutes. The balls' tumbling action wears down the manufacturer-added starch that makes them uncomfortable. The result: a soft, worn-in feel and a figure-flattering fit.

The no-fuss way to outfox wrinkles

WHEN YOUR PARTY DRESS is so creased that it looks like used tinfoil, set your dryer to the air cycle and pop in the dress, along with a damp towel, for 20 minutes. Unlike ironing, this nifty trick keeps your hands free so you can apply your makeup or do your hair. Meanwhile, the towel's moisture relaxes wrinkles so your dress can really do you justice!

The zipper trick that eliminates embarrassment

TO MAKE SURE A SLIDE-PRONE SKIRT ZIPPER STAYS PUT (and avert a red-faced moment), spray it lightly with hairspray after you've zipped it up. This coats the teeth with just enough sticky stuff to ensure the zipper stays right where it should be.

Remove melted crayon from clothes

YOU FORGOT TO CHECK the kids' pockets when you did the laundry, and now your favorite shirt has a blue crayon mark. The fix? Dab the spot with WD-40 and let sit for 10 minutes. Next, use a toothbrush to work ¹/₂ teaspoon dish soap into the stain, then rinse with hot water. The lubricant disintegrates the crayon particles as the soap dissolves any remaining greasy wax, leaving the shirt spotless!

So long, yellow teeth!

USING YOUR FINGERS OR THE BACK OF A SPOON, mash a strawberry into pulp and spread it over your teeth. Leave it on for two minutes, then rinse and brush as usual. The concentration of natural acid in strawberries acts as a mild bleaching agent, erasing food, tea, and coffee stains that can dull teeth and leaving you with a beautiful bright smile that will wow the world.

A drip-dry rack that won't collapse

ONCE YOUR LITTLE WANDERER outgrows the need for a safety gate, give it new life in the laundry room. Lean it against a wall and hang delicates that can't go in the dryer. Then simply tuck away.

Outsmart necklace knots

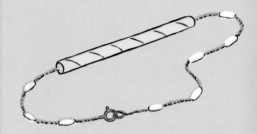

FORGET SPENDING MONEY ON A JEWELRY ORGANIZER to keep long chains and tiny clasps from becoming a jumbled mess—just use plastic drinking straws instead. Simply cut a straw in half, then thread a necklace through; fasten the clasp and arrange in your jewelry box. The straw ensures that each necklace lays taut so it won't become tangled with your other jewelry, allowing you to pick the perfect accessory every time.

Soothe an itchy scalp

DRY AIR FROM INDOOR HEATING can leave your scalp itchy and irritated. Instead of using specially formulated shampoo, massage 3/4 cup lemon juice into your scalp before you shower. Let sit for five minutes, then rinse and shampoo as usual. The juice's citric acid acts as an astringent to whisk away dead skin cells and kill *propionibacterium acnes*, the bacteria that clog sebaceous glands, so your skin can release scalp oils that moisturize and stop itching instantly.

Spiff up suede— for a song!

BREATHE NEW LIFE into your favorite well-worn suede jacket or skirt—without having to spend a fortune on dry cleaning—by trying this: Ball up a clean pair of panty hose and use a circular motion to give the garment a thorough rubdown. The positively charged nylon fibers attract and pick up negatively charged dust particles while the gentle rubbing action revives the nub, leaving the suede looking as good as the day you bought it.

SOS for stuck-on gum

WHEN YOUR LITTLE ONE'S BUBBLE GUM ends up on his shirt or your rug, fill a resealable plastic sandwich bag with ice and apply it to the sticky spot for 10 minutes. As gum gets cold, it shrinks and hardens, making it easy to peel off and toss away without damaging fabric.

Perfect bangs every time

BADLY BEHAVING BANGS making mornings a struggle? Try this styling trick: Set your blow-dryer on low and hold it just above your hairline so it aims straight down. Directing the airflow downward over damp strands forces a wayward fringe to lay flat, allowing you to step out the door knowing it's going to be a great hair day!

Maximize your mascara

Soak nearly empty tubes of liquid eyeliner and mascara in hot water for a few minutes before using. The heat dissolves product that has become stuck to the insides of the containers, guaranteeing you get to use every last pricey bit.

Whirl your way to longer, lusher lashes

BEFORE APPLYING MASCARA, briskly roll the tube between your palms for 20 seconds. You'll generate heat that dissolves clumps, so mascara goes on smoothly and evenly, creating beautiful, full lashes that make you even more magnetic.

Rid tar from shoes— instantly!

Skip THE FRUSTRATION of scraping at your sneaker soles when hot road tar gets lodged in their tiny grooves. Instead, rub the surface with a quarter-size dollop of petroleum jelly. The jelly binds to and softens tar on contact, so the gunk slides off before it has a chance to turn your smile upside down.

Discover your perfect fall fragrance

Before you visit the perfume counter
to trade your light summer scent for a
bolder autumn one, pick up a coffee to
go. Then as you test different perfumes,
refresh your nose by taking a sip or sniff
of the brew between spritzes. By introducing a different type of odor, you reset
scent receptors in the nose, so you're
better able to detect the notes and nuances
that make a fragrance an ideal fit for you.

The fountain
of youth
in your fridge

POUR A CUP OF APPLE JUICE into your bath for a
rejuvenating soak.
The malic acid in
apples is a natural
exfoliant that
sloughs off dead
skin cells.

Fade-proof bright garments

WHEN LAUNDERING BOLD-COLORED CLOTHING for the first time, toss 1 tablespoon salt into the washing machine. The chloride in salt seals pigment into fibers so colors won't run or bleed.

Freshen fine washables— for less

INSTEAD OF SPENDING BIG BUCKS on detergents for delicates, handwash them in $1/2$ cup baking soda mixed in $1/2$ cup warm water. The baking soda deodorizes without harming fragile fibers, so clothes come out fresh and clean.

Natural wart evaporator

CUT A DIME-SIZE PIECE from a banana peel, place it pulp side down on the wart and cover it with a bandage to hold in place overnight. Remove it in the morning. Apply a fresh peel nightly until the wart disappears—usually in about 14 days. The pulp contains mucilage, which kills the wart without harsh chemicals so skin heals flawlessly.

Effortless polish removal

WHEN POLISH REMOVER FAILS to erase every last trace of color, dissolve a denture-cleaning tablet in a cup of water, then soak your fingertips in the solution for 10 minutes. The bleaching agents in the tablet break down and remove the leftover hue, leaving your nails looking naturally beautiful.

Denture Tablet

Keep sunburned skin from peeling

IF A DAY SPENT POOLSIDE has left you with a stinging sunburn, don't bother buying after-sun lotion. Simply slice an apple in half, remove the core, and rub the fleshy side over the affected area for three minutes. The malic acid in this fruit-bowl favorite moisturizes over-sunned skin to keep it from blistering and peeling, so it heals faster.

Remove
lipstick stains

To wipe away a lipcolor smudge from a washable fabric (like cotton or rayon), immediately cover the stain with a dab of petroleum jelly. Let it sit for five minutes, then wash as usual. The jelly contains glycerin, which gently breaks down the oil-based stain without damaging the fabric. Your garment will look as good as new in no time!

Rub out collar stains

RID YOUR WHITE BLOUSES OF THOSE YELLOW RINGS that form on the collar with white chalk. Rub a generous amount of the powder briskly over the problem area, let sit for 10 minutes, then launder as usual. The chalk absorbs the sebum oil that holds in dirt and causes the ring, so the stains wash away easily.

Give stubborn knots the slip

SPRINKLE SHOELACES WITH TALCUM POWDER to untangle a tricky knot. The powder works its way between the shoelace fibers, lubricating and loosening the locked-up laces for easier untying.

Quick save for stretched-out cuffs

YOUR FAVORITE SWEATER—the one that flattens your belly and enhances your curves—has gotten a lot of wear. But there's no need to retire it just because the sleeves have stretched out. Simply spritz the cuffs with a spray bottle filled with hot water, then blow-dry. The combination of heated water and air causes natural fabrics (like wool, cotton, and linen) to shrink to their original shape. Your top will fit perfectly and you won't have to spend a cent to dry-clean it.

Easy bracelet fastening

STOP WRESTLING WITH A BRACELET that slides off while you're trying to snap it into place. Instead, secure one end to your wrist with a piece of clear tape, fasten the clasp with your other hand, then gently remove the tape. This way, you avoid getting frustrated and shave precious minutes off your get-ready routine.

Post-waxing redness reducer

BRING A BOTTLE OF EYEDROPS to your next brow wax. When finished, put three squirts of the drops on your finger and smooth over the irritated area. The tetrahydrozoline in eyedrops constricts capillaries, making redness disappear. You'll be able to show off your perfectly groomed eyebrows to the world worry-free.

Iron-free fix for hanger bumps

IT FIGURES. YOU'RE IN A RUSH and your favorite blouse is sporting "shoulder bumps." The quick fix? Just sprinkle the offending areas with warm water. Then, holding the shirt in one hand, set a blow-dryer on high and direct the airflow at the fabric. (Make sure to keep the dryer moving so the bumpy spots get hot but not scorched.) The heat loosens the warped fibers so the fabric settles back into its original, figure-flattering shape.

Smooth legs right now!

RUB A THIN LAYER OF CONDITIONER on your legs in the shower, let sit three minutes, then shave. The steam reacts with the glycerin and other oil extracts in the conditioner to moisturize skin and soften leg hair, so your blade glides easily. That means razor burn is history—and you emerge with beautiful, bare-able legs.

30 seconds to gorgeous skin

SOAK A WASHCLOTH IN HOT WATER, wring it out, and drape it over your face for 30 seconds. Remove, then cleanse your skin as usual and rinse with cool water. The steam helps cleanser dissolve the deepest clogs by opening pores, then the cool water seals them again, leaving you with a beautifully clear complexion.

Dissolve sweat stains

IF YOU FIND YOURSELF constantly buying new work shirts to replace your sweat-stained ones, try this: Combine 1 tablespoon ammonia and $1/2$ cup water. Rub the yellow marks with a sponge soaked in the solution, then launder as usual. Ammonia's alkaline nature neutralizes the stain-causing acids in sweat while dissolving unsightly oil and salt buildup, leaving shirts in like-new condition.

Boil your diamonds dazzling

FOR A BRILLIANT SHINE, place dull diamonds in a small pot filled with 1 cup water. Add 1 teaspoon dishwasher detergent and bring to a boil. Turn off heat; let pot sit until no longer warm to the touch. Once cool (no sooner or diamonds could crack) use tongs to remove the jewels. Rinse to get rid of residue.

So long, stinky sneakers!

PLACE SMELLY SHOES in resealable plastic bags and toss in the freezer overnight. The icy temperature kills odor-causing bacteria so you can change or slip off shoes anywhere, anytime without the faintest worry!

Eliminate bloodstains in seconds

WHEN A PESKY CUT or menstrual mayhem stains your light-colored outfit minutes before you're due at a party, this strategy will save the day: Simply remove the garment, rinse the stain with cold water, then dab the area with a clean cloth soaked in hydrogen peroxide until the mark disappears. The bleaching agent reacts with blood to break down stains instantly, so afterward all you have to do is blow-dry the area, slip the spot-free clothing back on, and head out to celebrate in style.

"Just washed" hair—instantly!

WHEN THERE'S NO TIME TO SHAMPOO, sprinkle 1 tablespoon sea salt onto dry hair (2 tablespoons if your hair falls below your shoulders) and massage with your fingers from scalp to ends. Leave it on for 15 minutes—or as long as it takes to apply your makeup or eat breakfast—then brush it out. The coarse crystals absorb excess oil and product residue, so you get a relaxed start to your busy day.

Break in new shoes in a snap

TAKE THE PAIN OUT OF breaking in new leather footwear with rubbing alcohol. Pour alcohol on a cotton ball and dab it on areas inside the shoe that pinch. Rubbing alcohol makes leather more pliable, so the shoe can conform more easily to the shape of your foot.

Look all-day radiant in 3 minutes

Use Pepto-Bismol as an instant cleansing mask. With a cotton ball, apply a thin layer of the pink stuff to your forehead, nose, cheeks, and chin. Let it sit for three minutes (or until dry), rinse with warm water, and pat dry. Bismuth, a claylike mineral in the liquid, acts as a cleansing agent to draw impurities out of the skin.

Save shirts from slipping

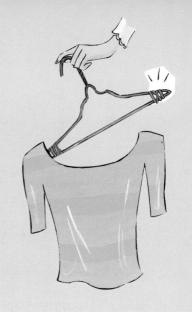

To keep wide-neck shirts from falling off their hangers and onto the closet floor, wrap rubber bands around the ends of your hangers. The cloth "grabs" the nonskid surface, so the shirts stay put.

The packing trick that keeps pants crease-free

TO PREVENT YOUR FAVORITE PAIR of trousers from wrinkling in your suitcase, try this: Before packing anything else, fold the pants in half and lay the top half in the bottom of your suitcase, letting the bottom half hang over the side. Place the rest of your clothes on top, then drape your trousers over the pile of clothes. Your pants will stay crisp and ready to wear.

Fast cure for cold sores

IF A COLD SORE HAS GOT YOU DOWN, place a brewed black tea bag in the freezer for 10 minutes, then hold it on the affected area for 3 minutes. The tannic acid in the tea reduces inflammation, while the cold sensation slightly numbs the area to alleviate discomfort. The impressive results will have you flashing that winning smile again!

Help for a home-color mishap

IF YOUR HOME HAIR-COLORING experiment leaves you with locks that are less than perfect, don't fret. Just wash your hair once or twice with a strong dandruff shampoo. The zinc pyrithione in the suds erases mistakes by opening cuticles, allowing hair to release color so you're left looking gorgeous!

Gorgeous sweaters (minus mothballs)

WHEN STORING WINTER WOOLENS, place each item in a plastic bag, lay a perfume sample from a magazine on top and seal. Since moths are instinctively drawn to the smell of wool, the fragrance acts like a repellent by masking the fabric's scent. Bonus: Come fall, your sweaters will smell sophisticated, not mildewy!

Lift tomato stains in just seconds

To remove a tomato-sauce stain from your favorite blouse, immediately apply a dollop of shaving cream to the area and dab with a damp sponge. Add a few drops of warm water to the spot, rub gently, let dry, then launder as usual. Shaving cream contains deionized water and alcohol, which help dissolve the stain without damaging clothes.

De-sap hands in a snap!

Dab a bit of baby oil on areas covered with tree sap, then rinse with warm water. The oil mixes with the sticky stuff so it "slides" off your skin easily.

Fast-acting blister balm

DIP A COTTON SWAB IN MOUTHWASH and
apply to broken blisters when you don't
have hydrogen peroxide on hand. The
mild antiseptic prevents infection and
promotes fast healing, allowing you to
step lively—and look lovely.

Powder multiplier

IF YOU LOVE LOOSE FACIAL POWDER, buy a hue that is one shade too dark for your complexion, then mix with unscented white baby powder until you achieve just the perfect shade. In the end, you'll have four times as much makeup.

Freshen up smoky clothes

INSTEAD OF PAYING THE DRY CLEANER every time an evening out leaves your wool jacket smelling like an ashtray, hang it over a tub half-filled with hot water and 3 cups white vinegar for a half hour. The vinegar-scented steam permeates fiber molecules, neutralizing lingering odors so clothes smell fresh and are ready to wear the very next day.

Simple
threading trick

Spritz the end of your thread with spray starch
or hairspray to make it stiff—
and easier to pass through the
eye of the needle.

Save time searching for earrings

SICK OF PAWING THROUGH your jewelry box to find a missing earring? Store them in spare buttons! Simply thread earrings through the button holes to keep them together and easy to find.

Erase pesky deodorant streaks

TRY THIS QUICK FIX for those stubborn white marks that just won't wipe off: Dab the area with a sponge soaked in one part white vinegar and one part water. (Just test a small area first in case it fades the fabric.) The acid in the vinegar loosens buildup of the deodorant's aluminum chloride, dissolving the stains on contact.

Mend bent sunglasses with this secret

EVER PULL YOUR SUNGLASSES out of the glove compartment to find the rims completely twisted? Don't toss the shades. Instead, repair them with a blow-dryer. Simply turn the dryer on high and blast hot air on the frames. The heat makes the plastic flexible so you'll be able to gently mold the glasses back to their original form!

Chapter 3

Kitchen & Bath

WHEN IT COMES TO HOUSEHOLD WOES, no two rooms have the potential for disaster like the kitchen and the bathroom. Whether it's a crack in the china or oversalted soup, a dripping faucet or a clogged showerhead, these tips will help fix minor disasters and prevent new ones from popping up. So the next time you have a dinner party or weekend guests, you can relax knowing the kitchen and bath are under your command. You might even teach your mother a thing or two!

No cork? No problem!

IT HAPPENS: AFTER HOSTING A STELLAR COCKTAIL PARTY, you find that you're left with a half-empty bottle of wine with a missing or broken cork. The fix? Soften an unscented taper candle in the microwave for three seconds; using a knife, cut an inch off the bottom and insert it into the bottle's opening. The pliable wax effortlessly seals the container. And when you're ready to finish the vino, simply pull out the wax like you would a cork.

De-wrinkle a vinyl tablecloth

SET YOUR BLOW-DRYER ON HIGH and hold it about eight inches away, directing the air over the wrinkled area. When the plastic begins to feel soft and pliable, smooth out the creases with your hand.

Erase baked-on oven grime in a snap!

TO REMOVE FOOD THAT IS STUCK to the oven's inner surface, apply a paste of $1/2$ cup baking soda and 2 tablespoons water. Let sit 10 minutes, then rub with a damp cloth. Baking soda's alkaline property dissolves gunk, while its abrasives make it possible to wipe away grime—without using any elbow grease!

Seal fine china cracks

PLACE THE CRACKED PIECE in a pot, cover with 2 cups milk, and simmer on the stovetop over low heat for 45 minutes. The milk protein casein expands when heated, filling in the fissures, then it bonds with the damaged portion of the china as it cools to restore its flawless finish.

Whisk away
pesky food odors

WHEN YOU'VE BEEN COOKING with fish, garlic, or onions and the odor lingers on your hands even after you've washed up, rub them with a stainless-steel spoon under cold running water. The sulfur from the foods is attracted to and binds with the metals in steel, drawing the sharp odors out of your skin so your hands smell fresh in a flash!

Dissolve dishwasher stains in a snap

ERASE YELLOW SPOTS (and mystery smells) from the dishwasher just in time for your mother-in-law's visit with this trick: Once the machine is empty, add a .14-ounce packet of citrus-flavored drink mix to the detergent cup, then run a normal cycle. The acid in the powder acts as a mild bleach to dissolve mold, ensuring you win Mom's approval—with no muss or fuss.

Make a scorched pot new again

MORNING SCHEDULE SO HECTIC that the coffee pot is left on the burner too long? Instead of scrubbing away the burn marks, use this waiter's trick: Once the pot has cooled, fill it halfway with ice, add ¼ cup salt, and swish it around for a minute or two. The friction created by the cubes and crystals dislodges stains, leaving the pot super-clean and ready for another round!

Never wrestle with plastic wrap again

STORE CELLOPHANE WRAP IN THE FREEZER.
The cold air reduces the plastic's static
electricity, so it won't stick to the roll (or
your hands) when you pull
off a piece. You'll be
able to seal leftovers
so they're airtight
without wasting
time struggling
with the wrap.

No more drive-you-crazy drips

IF A DRIPPING FAUCET IS KEEPING YOU UP ALL NIGHT, tie a piece of string to the faucet nozzle, resting the other end in the drain. The water will slowly flow down the length of the absorbent strand, silencing the maddening drip and saving your sanity until you can get it fixed.

Scrub-free secret to a clean blender

THERE'S NO NEED TO DISASSEMBLE a blender to wash it. Simply fill it halfway with warm water, add a drop of dishwashing liquid, and run it on low for about 30 seconds. The blending action does the dirty work, so all you need to do is pour out the sudsy solution and rinse with water to get your blender gleaming!

Easy egg saver

DON'T PITCH THOSE EGGS simply because their expiration date has passed. Test them first with this no-risk trick: Drop the suspect into a cup of water mixed with 2 teaspoons salt. If the egg sinks, it's still fresh. If it floats, it's bad—you'll have to toss it.

Quick pickup for baking spills

NEED A FAST, EASY WAY to whisk away sugar or sprinkles that have spilled on the floor during a cookie-baking marathon? Keep a lint roller on hand. Then simply glide over the hard-to-get mess and watch the sticky paper pick up every last particle, saving you from having to pinch them up with your fingers.

Prevent minor picnic knife mishaps

TOSS A FEW OLD WINE CORKS into your picnic basket, where they will come in handy when you need to transport paring knives. Simply make a vertical slit down the length of two corks and slide the blade into the openings. The makeshift sheath will prevent the sharp knife from poking into anything and keeps fingers (big and little ones) safe, ensuring a tranquil outdoor feast.

Speed-clean silver for a song!

IF YOU FIND THAT YOUR SILVERWARE IS TARNISHED just before your big holiday feast, don't bother polishing each piece. Instead, close your sink's drain and cover the bottom with a large sheet of aluminum foil (shiny side up). Fill the basin with hot water and add ¼ cup each salt and baking soda. Soak tarnished silver in the solution for 3 minutes before removing and drying. The electrolytes in the salt bath cause oxygen molecules to break their bonds with the silver and form stronger bonds with the aluminum, leaving silverware with a like-new sheen.

Freezer burn—foiled!

PROTECT FROZEN TREATS from those icky ice particles with aluminum foil. Simply cover your ice cream or sorbet container with a piece of foil, then put the lid on top. The thin metal sheet insulates your favorite cold treat from the moisture that causes freezer burn.

Make the most of leftover wine

DON'T POUR THE LAST OF THE WINE DOWN THE DRAIN— instead, freeze it in an ice-cube tray. Then when you need to add zip to soups and sauces, just pop and drop!

A grime-free fridge top

RATHER THAN CLIMB, stretch, and strain to clean the dirt from the top of your refrigerator, cover the area with a piece of plastic wrap. Then simply replace it with a fresh sheet once a month.

en appliances
without painting

ELIMINATE YELLOWING by making your own bleaching solution. Add $1/2$ cup bleach and $1/4$ cup baking soda to 4 cups warm water. Dip a cloth in the liquid and wipe appliances. Leave on for 10 minutes, then buff with a dry soft cloth to restore sparkle and shine.

Pop corn into the freezer for perfect kernels

TIRED OF FINDING UNPOPPED KERNELS at the bottom of the popcorn bag? Store your popcorn in a sealed container in the freezer. The cold helps kernels retain the moisture they need to pop light and fluffy.

SOS for a sticky can opener

IF YOU'RE HAVING TROUBLE turning a manual can opener, simply insert the edge of a 3-inch wide strip of wax paper between the blades and turn the handle as usual. The paper creates friction that whisks away rust and grime while the wax coating lubricates the blades and wheels, so slicing through can lids is always a breeze.

Decorate cakes like a pro

FOR GOOF-PROOF INSCRIPTIONS on your homemade cake, create a template by writing your message with a toothpick. Then go over it with icing. The grooves left by the pick will help the icing stay put.

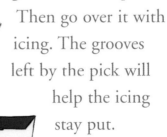

Fast fix for pizza burn

WHEN YOU'VE SCORCHED THE ROOF OF YOUR MOUTH by biting into piping-hot pizza, ease the pain by drinking a glass of milk. The cold liquid soothes the burn, while the protein in the beverage coats the sore, creating a protective barrier that prevents further injury so you can enjoy the rest of your slice.

Ice-cold drinks in a blink!

TO QUICKLY CHILL room-temperature bottled beverages for a barbecue, place them in a cooler, pack a layer of ice around the bases and sprinkle with a few tablespoons of salt. Continue to layer the ice and salt until all the bottlenecks are covered, then fill the cooler with water. The salt causes a temperature drop in the cooler that ensures drinks get frosty in a flash.

Spot-proof your potholders

SIMPLY SPRITZ YOUR POTHOLDERS with starch every other time you use them. The starch repels grease, so potholders stay stain-free.

De-cork wine without a corkscrew

NEED TO OPEN A BOTTLE OF WINE but there's no corkscrew around? Simply run the neck of the bottle under very hot water for two minutes. The heat causes the glass to contract slightly— just enough to force the cork partially out of the bottle's neck—so all you have to do is give it a quick tug.

The secret to super-flaky piecrusts

TO KEEP DOUGH FROM STICKING to your rolling pin, slip a clean knee-high stocking with the toe cut off over the roller and dust with flour before using. The nylon holds on to the flour so dough stays put.

Keep cookies extra-chewy

ADD A SLICE OF BREAD to your cookie jar (white, wheat   it doesn't matter) before you fill it. The bread absorbs moisture from the cookies, so they retain their chewy freshness without turning mushy.

Fog-proof bathroom mirrors

WANT A CLEAN AND CLEAR BATHROOM MIRROR after showering? Squirt a small dab of shaving cream onto a paper towel, rub it over the glass, then wipe with a dry cloth. The cream leaves an invisible film, making it difficult for water beads to stick and giving you a fog-free mirror for weeks.

Fizz away toilet rings

To whisk away unsightly buildup in your toilet, drop a denture tablet in the bowl once a month. Let it sit overnight, then flush. The effervescent compounds in the tablet loosen particles, while the oxidant ingredients work to polish the porcelain. The result: Your bowl is left gleaming—without the work!

Outsmart rust rings

PREVENT UNWANTED RUST on cabinet shelves when storing metal cans by placing them on old margarine tub tops. The plastic lids act as coasters, so rust collects on them—not your shelves.

Stain-guard your food-storage tubs

BEFORE POURING RICHLY COLORED FOODS, like tomato-based sauces or curries, into plastic containers, lightly coat the insides with nonstick cooking spray. The oil and lecithin (a waxy compound) in the spray form a protective barrier that repels stain-setting pigments, so your storage tubs stay looking new.

Silence squeaky shower curtain rings

INSTEAD OF PUTTING UP WITH a shower curtain that squeaks every time you move it, use a soft, dry cloth to apply 2 tablespoons car wax to the entire curtain rod. Gently buff with the same cloth to remove any excess lubricant. The silicone and wax in the polish form a slick, invisible coating that allows the curtain rings to slide effortlessly and silently across the metal bar.

Keep Spot safe (and your toilet sparkling)

WORRIED YOUR PUP WILL GET SICK from bowl cleaner when he drinks out of the toilet? Instead, sprinkle 2 tablespoons orange-flavored drink crystals into the water and swish with a brush. Close the lid and let sit overnight, then flush. The drink mix's citric acid dissolves grime, guaranteeing gleaming porcelain and a safe pet.

So long, burnt cupcake drips

LINE MUFFIN TINS with paper baking cups, then fill with cupcake batter using a turkey baster. You'll hit the mark every time so pans emerge from the oven sans baked-on bits. Plus, you'll sidestep drips that burn and smell up your kitchen. To clean, simply rinse and dry the tins (no soap or elbow grease required)!

Get the best from your garbage disposal

KEEP YOUR DISPOSAL RUNNING SMOOTHLY and smelling sweet by grinding vinegar "ice" cubes every few weeks. Simply grind six cubes for 15 seconds and flush with water. The ice sharpens blades and dislodges dried food, while the acetic acid in vinegar deodorizes. The result? No more disposal hassles!

Brighter tile grout in a blink

WHEN EVEN EXPENSIVE TILE CLEANERS leave your grout looking dingy, reach for soda. Using a toothbrush, apply cola to the affected areas. Allow it to sit for 10 minutes, then wipe away with a soapy cloth. The phosphoric acid in the beverage fizzes and seeps into the mortar, dissolving embedded stains and restoring the concrete to its whitest.

Set-in-place shelf liners

INSTEAD OF STRUGGLING with cumbersome shelf paper, line kitchen cupboards with inexpensive peel-and-stick linoleum floor tiles (about 50 cents per square foot). Just cut them to size (the 12-inch squares require minimal measuring), peel off the backing and set in place— no muss and much less fuss.

See ya, smelly microwave

WHEN STRONG-SMELLING FOODS, like fish, leave a lingering odor in your microwave, neutralize it in minutes: Combine the juice of 1 lemon with 1 cup water in a microwave-safe bowl and place in the oven. Bring to a boil (times vary according to model), then let sit 10 minutes for a lemon-fresh scent.

Unblock a clogged showerhead

NO NEED TO DISASSEMBLE A SHOWERHEAD to clear a clog. Simply pour a cup of white vinegar into a small plastic bag. Secure the bag around the showerhead with duct tape and let the head soak overnight. The acid in the vinegar dissolves mildew and soap scum, allowing water to flow freely again. (For brass fixtures, dilute 1 part vinegar with 10 parts water to avoid tarnishing.)

Eliminate cooler odor overnight

IF THE SCENT OF LAST MONTH'S HOT DOGS lingers in your cooler, leave a small bowl of charcoal in the closed box overnight. The next day, remove the bowl and wash the cooler with soapy water. Charcoal's porous nature enables it to absorb moisture that causes odors, leaving your cooler fresh-scented and ready to go for the next neighborhood cookout!

Keep recipes at your fingertips (and away from splatters)

Instead of thumbing through boxes of recipe cards, organize your favorites in a photo album with clear sleeves that let you see the front and back of each recipe. You'll find what you need in seconds, plus the plastic protects recipes from spills and splatters while you cook.

Eliminate shower curtain mold for good

PREVENT MOLD FROM FORMING on your plastic shower curtain liner by trimming the bottom with pinking shears, sewing scissors designed to prevent fabric from unraveling when cut. The zigzag hem it creates gives water more places to drip off, which speeds drying time and erases lingering moisture that promotes mildew formation.

The screwdriver in your kitchen drawer

IF YOU NEED TO EXTRACT a Phillips-head screw but don't have a Phillips screwdriver on hand, use a metal potato peeler instead. The curved top edge fits perfectly into the star-shaped grooves of the screw head, so loosening it is a breeze.

The throwaway that gets showers gleaming

WHEN YOUR SHOWER DOORS ARE COVERED with soap scum and you don't have time to run out for cleaner before your guests arrive, try this: Wet a dryer sheet and use it to scrub the doors. Lubricants in the laundry staple loosen the scum's bond to surfaces, while the sheet's woven texture scrubs away grime.

Add sparkle to copper

BUFF COPPER SURFACES with a lemon half dipped in salt. Then rinse and dry the copper with a clean soft cloth. Lemon's citric acid instantly dissolves tarnish, while the salt grains scour it away to reveal shine.

Fast rescue for a cork uh-oh

IF YOU OPEN A BOTTLE OF WINE and the cork breaks, pour it through a coffee filter to catch stray pieces before serving it to guests.

No-tears onion peeling

BEFORE YOU PEEL OR SLICE RAW ONIONS, light a match. The sulfur disables the compounds in onions that make you cry, so you can harness all the wonderful flavor without getting weepy.

Icing made simple

To keep a cake from sliding around while you slather on icing, drop a dollop of frosting in the middle of a plate and set the cake on top. The frosting acts as a glue so the cake stays put, letting you decorate with ease.

Keep shower drains running clear

IF CLOG-PRONE DRAINS leave you standing in a shallow pool of water by shower's end, try this: Pour a packet or two of active dry yeast and a pinch of sugar down the drain, then run warm water for 15 seconds. This causes live cultures in the yeast to reproduce and expand, which breaks apart stubborn hair clogs and grime to keep your drain blockage-free.

New life for leftover spuds

Drop spoonfuls of leftover mashed potatoes on a baking sheet, freeze, remove and store in a resealable plastic bag in the freezer. They last for up to two months and are the perfect size to pop into soup or stew.

Quick save for salty soup

WHEN A TASTE TEST REVEALS you've added too much salt to soup or stew, just drop in a couple extra diced peeled potatoes to soak up the excess. And if your recipe doesn't call for potatoes, cube them instead of dicing so you can easily scoop them out when the dish is done.

Chapter 4

Home & Garden

IF YOU FEEL MORE LIKE A BUNGLING ROOKIE than a smart cookie when it comes to household chores, read up on these pointers to become a pro in no time. With these bits of advice, you'll learn how to solve irksome problems like wax spatters on a tablecloth and a slow-running lawnmower, and make those weekend chores—like hanging pictures or winterizing a car battery—a snap.

Avoid stiff paintbrush bristles

To take a break from a painting project without worrying about your brush drying out, wrap it in a plastic bag and place in the freezer. The cold temperature keeps the liquid components of paint from evaporating and hardening the bristles.

Refresh silk flowers— in two shakes

SILK FLOWERS LOOKING A LITTLE DULL?
Pour a cup of salt into a one-gallon
plastic bag, then place three flowers
inside at a time. Seal the bag and shake
for 30 seconds. The salt grains act as
an exfoliant, dislodging dirt from the
smallest crevices and restoring the flowers'
beauty in moments.

Dodge pesky grass stains

BEFORE KNEELING TO WEED your garden, tie a plastic grocery bag around each knee. These makeshift kneepads act as a barrier between the fabric and the soil, plus they add extra cushioning to protect your joints.

So long, wax splatters!

INSTEAD OF SCRAPING candle spills off your coffee table and risking a damaged finish, melt the wax with a hair dryer set on low and wipe it up with a paper towel. Then apply 1 teaspoon vinegar to a damp sponge and wipe the area. The heat softens wax so it can easily be mopped up, while the vinegar's acetic acid dissolves any remaining residue.

Prevent an icy windshield

WHEN THE WEATHERMAN predicts overnight ice, try this to ensure a quick getaway come morning: Place two old bath towels across the windshield and tuck them under the wipers to secure. The towels keep ice and snow from accumulating. The next day you simply pull them off, shake out the ice and hang them in the garage before going on your way!

Winterize your car battery

COLD, HARSH WEATHER can corrode car-battery posts (the metal terminals where jumper cables are clamped), hampering the battery's performance. To ensure you'll never be stuck with a vehicle that won't start, take this step before temperatures plummet: Pour a 12-ounce can of cola over posts; let sit for 15 minutes, then wipe clean and dry. Next, rub a coat of lip balm over the posts. The phosphoric acid in soda dissolves any preexisting rust, while the petroleum jelly in lip balm seals out corrosion-causing moisture and oxygen.

Lint-trap trick that cuts costs

IF YOUR DRYER IS TAKING LONGER than usual to get the job done—and sending your electric bill sky-high—a sneaky accumulation of fabric-softener residue in the lint trap may be to blame. The remedy: Remove the trap and scrub with an old toothbrush dipped in a solution of 1 cup water and 2 tablespoons liquid dish detergent. Rinse well with warm water and replace. The soap's alkaline quality dissolves the gunk, restoring optimal airflow and water drainage in your machine so garments dry at top speed.

The ink-spot eraser
in your refrigerator

NO NEED TO PANIC if your pen nicks the arm of your leather chair as you jot down a note. Simply saturate the corner of a paper towel with milk and blot until the stain disappears. Then wipe clean with a damp sponge. The milk's enzymes break down the oil that bonds ink to the fabric. Plus, the milk's protein moisturizes the leather, making it as soft as ever.

Easy-as-pie pillow plumper

FORGET SPENDING HOURS VACUUMING and
fluffing pillows before visitors are due to
arrive. Instead, toss the decor pieces into
the dryer with two old tennis balls for
30 minutes. The heat and movement
of the dryer shake dust particles loose,
while the pounding of the tennis balls
plumps up the fabric and stuffing,
ensuring fresh cushions that will impress
even persnickety guests.

Skin-friendly paint remover

OUTDOOR TOUCH-UP WORK turned your skin into a canvas? Instead of using pungent turpentine to remove oil-based paint splatters, raid your cupboard for olive oil. Apply a drop directly to each spot, rub with a damp sponge and rinse with soapy water. The oil breaks down paint pigments so they easily disappear, minus the stench!

Guard your car against insect splats

SKIP THE PRICEY HEAVY-DUTY CLEANER and mix ½ cup baking soda with water to form a thick paste. Dab on the spots, let sit five minutes, rinse and rub dry. The water softens residue as the grainy powder abrades gunk—without marring your car's finish.

Avoid pinholed walls with this trick

IF YOUR DAUGHTER HANGS A NEW POSTER
of the latest teen idol on her bedroom
wall every other week, show her this
tip to sidestep pinholes: Dab white
toothpaste on each of the poster's corners
and stick onto the wall, applying light
pressure to the pasted areas. The cellulose
in the toothpaste binds the paper to
the wall, while the paste's glycerin keeps
it from losing its holding power. When
the picture comes down, simply wipe
away the leftover residue with a damp
soapy cloth.

Quick fix for stuck lightbulbs

RUB A DIME-SIZE DAB OF PETROLEUM JELLY over a new bulb's metal threads before twisting it into an outdoor fixture. The oil in the jelly forms a waterproof barrier that keeps the elements out and prevents rust from forming—and metal from expanding!

Never skid again!

WHEN YOUR CAR TIRES START TO GET WORN, find out if you need new ones with this trick: Insert a penny into the shallowest tread so that Lincoln's head is pointed toward the hubcap. If you can see the hair on top of his head, the tread is very worn down and it's time to buy a new tire. But if Abe's face just peeks out, the tire still has enough grip to keep you safe on the road.

The secret to stay-put dog dishes

WHEN YOU FIND YOURSELF tripping over Bowser's food and water bowls, try this trick: Snip six wide rubber bands (like the ones around broccoli stalks) with scissors to create flat strips, then superglue a few pieces across the bottom of each dish. The no-slip rubber surface creates friction between the dishes and the floor, keeping your pup from sliding (and slopping) his supper across the room.

The sprinkle that quiets a creaky floor

DON'T WORRY ABOUT WALKING on tiptoe so you don't wake the kids. Just use a turkey baster to apply talcum powder along the cracks between noisy floor-boards. The soft substance acts as a stopgap, preventing boards from shifting as you step.

Erase crayon marks in seconds

IF YOUR PINT-SIZE PICASSO creates a crayon masterpiece on your living-room wall, stir together 2 tablespoons baking soda and 1 teaspoon water until the mixture is the consistency of toothpaste. Using a damp white cloth, apply the mixture directly to marks and gently rub in a circular motion until they disappear. Soaplike compounds in baking soda dissolve coloring agents, while its mild abrasives buff away greasy crayon wax without damaging walls.

Revive potpourri instantly

IF YOUR FAVORITE POTPOURRI LOSES ITS SCENT too soon, simply pour ¼ cup vodka into a spray bottle and spritz liberally, then stir to saturate every piece. The odorless alcohol breaks down potpourri's hardened surface, exposing the still-strong-scented layers underneath, so your home smells sweet until spring.

Light a fire without risking a burn

IF YOU HAPPEN TO RUN OUT OF long matches for the fireplace, simply use a piece of raw spaghetti instead. It safely lets you reach the middle of the kindling and burns for so long that you'll even have time to light a few candles on the mantle without burning your fingertips.

Clean dolls on the double

ERASE DIRT, GRIME, AND INK MARKS from your daughter's favorite doll—and make her day—by smoothing a thin layer of peanut butter on Dolly's plastic face, arms or legs with a dry cloth. Leave it on for five minutes and wipe away with a damp soapy paper towel. The oil in peanut butter seeps into the porous plastic, attracting and lifting embedded dirt that scrubbing simply won't remove.

No more messy paw prints!

INSTEAD OF USING SOAP AND WATER to wash your pup's paws, save time and hassle by cleaning them with a few baby wipes. Simply swipe his soles and the areas between his digits to remove dried mud and dirt that would otherwise get tracked into your home.

Extract a broken key— for free

BEFORE SHELLING OUT MONEY for a locksmith when the key breaks in your front door, dab superglue onto the broken edge of the free piece. Next, slide it into the keyhole and press it firmly against the stuck half. Let dry for three minutes before removing the whole key. The glue fuses the two halves together so you can extract the broken piece in a cinch.

Keep windowsills dust-free

A RECENT STUDY FOUND that windowsills are the top spot for household mold and dust. Prevent allergens from settling on clean sills by rubbing the surface with a white candle. The wax film seals the trim and stops moisture and dirt from seeping into cracks, so you can breathe easy all summer!

Hammer without the hurt

IF YOU PUT YOUR FINGERS in harm's way every time you hammer a nail into the wall, just reach for a fork. Place the nail between the tines to keep it steady as you swing away—safely.

A freshly mowed lawn in half the time

IF IT SEEMS LIKE CUTTING THE GRASS is taking longer than usual, it could be that grass accumulation on the machine's underside is jamming the blades. Brush away buildup with a paintbrush, then spritz the metal with a light coat of nonstick cooking oil. The spray stops grass from adhering, preventing blockages and ensuring a perfectly manicured lawn in moments.

Sidestep paint-smell headaches

BEFORE APPLYING LATEX PAINT TO WALLS, add 1 tablespoons vanilla extract per pint, stir thoroughly and brush or roll on as usual. Vanilla reacts with chemicals in paint to curb the odor without affecting the pigment.

The dust buster that stops seasonal sniffles

INCESSANT INDOOR SNEEZING may be caused by dust particles hidden in hard-to-clean crevices of vents and radiators. To sniff them out, set your blow-dryer on low and direct the airflow in one direction (top to bottom for radiators, left to right for vents). Dust particles will accumulate in one spot for easy vacuum pickup.

Patch a torn screen with clear polish

IF PESKY INSECTS have buzzed their way into your home through a hole in a window screen, block their entrance in a blink by "mending" the space with a drop or two of clear nail polish.

Protect fine garments (minus stinky mothballs!)

IF YOUR CEDAR CHEST'S FRESH SCENT has faded, don't resort to mothballs. Just take a sheet of fine-grade sandpaper and give the wood inside the box a gentle once-over, making sure to go with the grain. This exposes the wood's moist and fragrant underlayer to protect and preserve your finery.

Bye-bye, dust bunnies!

TO QUICKLY CAPTURE DUST BUNNIES, bend a wire hanger to form a loop, stretch one leg of an old pair of panty hose over it and spritz with furniture polish. Swish it around hard-to-reach hideouts, like under the bed or fridge. The damp nylon acts as a dust magnet to ensure sneeze-free surroundings.

Defog any vase

WHEN YOUR FAVORITE VASE gets gunked up with plant residue, fill it with water—the hotter the better—then drop in two Alka-Seltzer tablets. The citric acid and sodium bicarbonate in the heartburn remedy create bubbles that break apart caked-on plant matter so the glass looks clean, clear, and worthy of your beautiful bouquets.

Double the life of a rose bouquet

THE GORGEOUS ARRANGEMENT OF ROSES that your sweetheart gives you every anniversary always wilts before you've had a chance to show it off. The remedy: Submerge the stems in a basin of hot water and trim $1/2$ inch off the ends. In their rush to fill Cupid's orders, florists tend to cut flowers in the open air, introducing air bubbles into the stems that prevent water from being fully absorbed. But the underwater snipping allows water to travel up to the buds with ease, so your beautiful blooms will garner oohs and ahhs for weeks.

Thwart trash bandits

KEEP RACCOONS, SQUIRRELS, and other pesky critters out of your garbage by spraying a little white vinegar on cans and bags. The pungent smell repels the four-legged foragers.

Tame heating bills with Teddy

LINE UP ALL YOUR CHILD'S STUFFED ANIMALS on the windowsill in her room to block cool drafts.

Slip-proof your front steps

YOU'LL DO ANYTHING TO PREVENT someone from having a nasty fall on your steps, but repeatedly salting them is time-consuming, and the chalky residue gets tracked into the house. For a no-fuss remedy, pour a solution of 1 gallon hot water and 2 tablespoons liquid soap over the stairs. The heat melts the ice, while the soap leaves behind water-repelling molecules that prevent liquid from refreezing for days.

The secret to perfectly placed pictures

SPARE YOUR WALLS from needless nail holes by tracing around artwork on brown paper bags before hanging. Then simply cut out the patterns and use masking tape to stick them on the wall. Rearrange until you're happy with the placement. Next, tap nails into the wall through the bags and tear away the paper. The result: gallery-gorgeous walls without a hassle.

Defog your windshield with a swipe

KEEP A BLACKBOARD ERASER in your glove compartment. Just a few quick swipes can remove the fog that obscures your vision without leaving behind streaks. Simply wipe, then safely pull out of your driveway without having to wait for your defroster to kick in.

Fingerprint-proof your walls

SPRITZ SPRAY STARCH on doors, hallway walls, banisters and other painted areas that get lots of hand traffic. The slick coating repels fingerprints and smudges, keeping surfaces pristine.

Cut shoveling time in half

BEFORE YOU HEAD OUTSIDE to tackle your winter woes, spread about a cup of shortening over the paddle of your shovel with an old rag. The fatty substance creates a water-resistant layer that stops snow from sticking to your shovel and weighing you down while you work. You'll do the job in half the time and keep your shovel rust-free.

Revive houseplants (for free!)

THE LIMITED SUNLIGHT of the winter months has left your plants looking droopy. But that doesn't mean you should spend a fortune on plant food (or new plants). The thrifty cure: Whenever you boil potatoes or pasta for dinner, strain the water into a second pot, let cool for at least one hour and use it the next time you feed your plants. The leftover starch in the water infuses soil with the complex sugars that the foliage needs to thrive.

Streaky windshields be gone!

WHEN YOUR WIPER BLADES begin to wear down, leaving your windshield a smeared mess, give them a quick swipe using a clean rag saturated with white vinegar. The liquid's acidic properties dissolve grime on contact, ensuring crystal-clear visibility during inevitable spring storms. Bonus: the vinegar will help your blades last longer.

Pick up glass shards in seconds

NEXT TIME A GLASS IS SHATTERED during dinner-party mayhem, use a slice of white bread to pick up hard-to-see splinters in a jiffy. Simply flick a bit of water onto the bread, then slowly wipe the floor with it, wet side down. The sticky, porous quality of the bread attracts and lifts the tiny shards that a broom misses, so the floor is clear—and safe—in a flash.

Take the pinch out of pruning

WHEN PRUNING A THORNY PLANT, like roses or holly, hold branches safely out of your way with a pair of kitchen tongs to prevent pricking your fingers or arms as you snip.

Fresh-smelling hands in a blink

AFTER GETTING THE HOUSE SPIC AND SPAN for the holidays, remove bleach and other cleaning-product odors from hands by washing them with lukewarm water and a little toothpaste. The paste's thick, mildly abrasive consistency scrubs away lingering scent molecules from the skin's surface, so your hands become minty-clean in minutes.

Pro tip for dusting edges

USE A CLEAN EMPTY SPRAY BOTTLE to dust intricately carved picture frames or any little nooks and crannies. Just direct the nozzle toward the fuzzy stuff and pump out air until the small particles blow away.

Fix for pesky carpet dents

PLACE AN ICE CUBE in the rug indentation. As it melts, the moisture sinks in and plumps up the fibers, so your carpet will become smooth and dent-free again.

Remove sticky labels in a snap

WANT TO BREAK OUT your new wine glasses but don't have time to scratch off each sticky label? Try this: combine equal parts white vinegar and lukewarm water in a basin, then soak the glassware for 10 minutes. The acetic acid in the solution dissolves adhesive and mineral deposits so the stickers practically peel themselves off!

Dissolve driveway oil stains for pennies!

FORGET SPENDING MONEY on pricey cleaners to erase driveway oil spots. Instead, sprinkle $1/2$ cup baking soda over marks and rub with a wet hard-bristled scrub brush. Baking soda's alkaline nature works like soap to break apart oil particles, while its abrasive qualities scour the concrete, removing the ugly spillage so your driveway is the spiffiest on the block.

Brighten aluminum blinds

MAKE SMUDGES on your aluminum blinds disappear by rubbing them with a soft pencil eraser. The rubber lifts unsightly marks just as easily as it erases graphite.

Sweeter-smelling doggy bed

CLEAN YOUR PET'S BED without having to launder it. Simply give it a good rubdown with a few baby wipes. They contain alcohol that destroys germs and leaves the bed smelling fresh (without harming Fido).

A clean sweep every time!

To keep a broom from leaving a tiny trail of dust in its wake, try this: Fill a spray bottle with a solution of $1/4$ cup liquid fabric softener and $3/4$ cup water, then lightly spritz the bristles just before sweeping. The solution makes the needles more pliable, which helps them attract and collect every speck of dust and pet hair that crosses their path, ensuring you never have to double back.

Freshen a musty garage

IF YOU'RE ABOUT TO SET UP your annual garage sale but humid weather has left the area smelling mustier than usual, try this trick: Spread a layer of cat litter in a shallow pan and place in an inconspicuous spot. The absorbent granules will soak up the moisture in the air that causes stale smells.

Clean out every lampshade crevice

To dust a delicate pleated lampshade, simply stroke it from top to bottom with a clean dry paintbrush. The needle-thin bristles easily fit into hard-to-reach creases, sweeping out dirt to leave your shade dust-free and looking good as new!

In-a-pinch
carpet cleaner

Out of rug-cleaning foam? Not a problem! Whether you have a wine spill or a light grease stain, just apply a dollop of shaving cream to the area and let sit for five minutes. Then scrape off the foam with a spatula, dab the spot with a wet cloth and vacuum as usual. Shaving cream contains glycerin, a compound that dissolves stains to leave your carpet spotless.

Make your sheets smell super-sweet

LOOKING FOR SOMETHING TO DO with the huge stash of bath salts you always receive as gifts but never use? Add $^1\!/_4$ cup to the rinse cycle of your washer (instead of fabric softener) when laundering linens and blankets. The same essential oils that scent bathwater are absorbed by the fabric's fibers to leave a long-lasting fragrance. Plus, the salts act like starch to ensure that sheets are extra crisp and clean.

Dissolve water stains overnight

WHEN GUESTS LEAVE unsightly water rings on your wooden furniture, rub 1/2 teaspoon mayonnaise directly onto the stains with a paper towel and let sit overnight. The next day, simply wipe with a clean damp cloth. The mayo soaks in and absorbs water from the marks, dissolving them and restoring the wood's natural luster.

Get more bang from your vacuum bags

INSTEAD OF THROWING AWAY A VACUUM BAG once it's full, hang onto it! Most bags are durable enough to be reused three or four times. Simply clip off the top of the full bag, dump out the debris, fold the top edge over once, then staple it closed.

Fido-proof your flower patch

STOP YOUR POOCH FROM DIGGING up your prized begonias by sprinkling a dash of cayenne pepper over his favorite burrowing spots. When Fido sticks his nose where it doesn't belong, the spice will tickle his nose hairs, making him sneeze. The memory of the sensation will remind him to keep away the next time he wants to dig, which guarantees your garden stays lush and lovely.

No more crooked pictures!

PREVENT HANGING MIRRORS AND PICTURE FRAMES from tilting this way and that while you dust by sticking corn cushions behind the corners. The pads help frames stay perfectly straight without damaging the wall's surface.

Glistening patio furniture

APPLY A LIGHT COAT OF CAR WAX before setting out your plastic or metal chairs for another season. The same slick stuff that keeps bugs from sticking to your hood will make furniture a breeze to clean and protect it from fading in the sun.

Clear away webs

TO CLEAR COBWEBS from hard-to-reach places without making a mess, cover the bristle end of your broom with a damp pillowcase, secure with a rubber band and swat. The webs cling to the moist fabric, which you can then easily toss into the wash.

Unstick
photos fast

To pull apart stuck-together snapshots, set your hair dryer on low and blow photos from six inches away. The heat loosens the adhesive in three minutes so you can gently separate them.

Freeze-proof car locks

TO PREVENT AN ICY CAR-DOOR LOCK from making you late, try this: Cut two large circles out of a flat magnet (the kind the pizza guy leaves). Place the pieces over the driver's-door and trunk keyholes at the end of each day. The magnet forms a seal that keeps water from getting in the lock and freezing. Come morning, slide off the circles and be on your way.

No-fuss fireplace cleanup

AFTER MAKING TEA, don't toss the bags—break them open and sprinkle over sooty fireplace remains before you sweep them up. The damp leaves settle the flaky ash particles, keeping them from rising—and making you cough—when you're cleaning.

Unstick a rusty screw

CAN'T GET THAT OLD HARDWARE on your daughter's too-low bike seat to budge? Just pour a capful of club soda over it to dissolve the rust and sediment that prevent it from turning. The carbon dioxide, which makes club soda and other soft drinks fizzy, bubbles the rust and dirt away so you can be sure your child's bike will be ready to roll in no time.

Bye-bye, jiggly doorknobs!

REMOVE LOOSE SCREWS from jiggly door-knobs and dip them in clear nail polish, let dry for about a minute, then screw them back into the knob. The sticky polish acts as an adhesive that makes the screws (and your doorknob) stay firmly in place!

Whisk away grease with soda

EMPTY ONE CAN OF LIGHT-COLORED SODA, like 7-Up, into a washing machine while it's filling, then toss in greasy clothes. Add detergent and run through a regular wash cycle. The soda's citric acid breaks down oils so they wash out of fabrics and down the drain.

First aid for furniture nicks

NEXT TIME YOUR LITTLE ONE rams his metal truck into your wooden coffee table and leaves a dent, place a wet rag on the spot and run an iron set on steam over it five times. The heat and moisture cause the wood fibers to swell and fill in the dent, restoring your table's flawless finish in no time.

Erase
furniture
scratches

Index

IF YOU NOTICE A SCRATCH on your wooden tabletop, don't despair! Just break a walnut, pecan, or Brazil nut in half, then wipe the mark with the nut's flesh in the direction of the nick. Next, rub your middle finger back and forth over the area until it is warm. The body heat makes the wood expand slightly to absorb the nut's oil, which fills in the nick and restores the table's sheen, ensuring a smooth finish in no time.